South Lanarkshire Street Atlas

CON

Area of Coverage	2 - 3
Lanark	4 - 5
Larkhall & Ashgill	6 - 9
Carluke	10 - 11
Lesmahagow & index	12 - 15
Biggar & index	16 - 17
Law & index	18 - 19
Stonehouse & index	20 - 21
Strathaven & index	22 - 23

	24 - 25
	26 - 27
	28 - 29
....ns & indices	30 - 31
..g, Blackwood, Kirkmuirhill & indices	32 - 33
Wanlockhead, Symington & indices	34 - 35
West End, Carnwath, Carstairs,	
Carstairs Junction & indices	36 - 37
Lanark, Larkhall & Carluke indices	38 - 42

KEY TO MAP SYMBOLS

—— M74 ——	Motorway	P F	Parking / filling station
—— A72 ——	A road dual / single carriageway	i	Tourist information centre
—— B743 ——	B road dual / single carriageway	⚔	Castle
	Unclassified road	m	Museum
	Track / path	a	Antiquity
	Railway / tunnel or disused railway	❀	Viewpoint
🚉	Railway station	✳	Other tourist attraction
P F A	Police / fire / ambulance station	▲	Camping
▲ ▼	Primary / secondary school	⊞	Caravan site
△	Special or independent school		Woodland
+ H	Place of worship / hospital		Park / recreation / cemetery
PO L	Post Office / library		Built up area

ISBN 1 86097 136 9

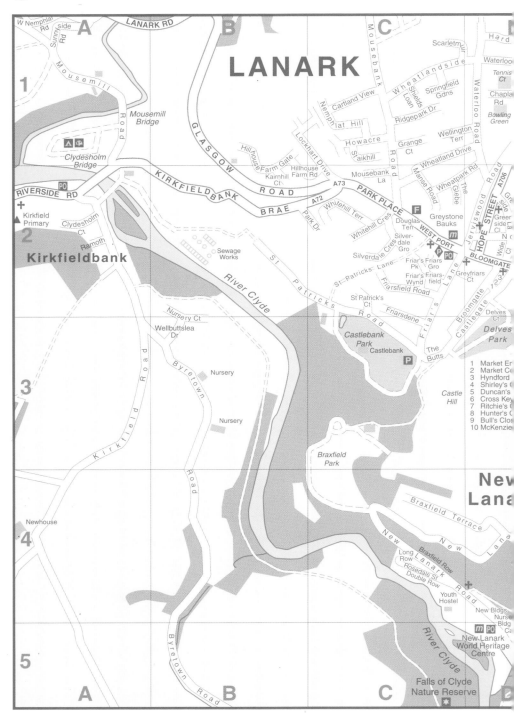

LANARK

Kirkfieldbank

New
Lana

New Lanark
World Heritage
Centre

Falls of Clyde
Nature Reserve

1 Market En
2 Market Co
3 Hyndford
4 Shirley's C
5 Duncan's
6 Cross Key
7 Ritchie's C
8 Hunter's C
9 Bull's Clos
10 McKenzie

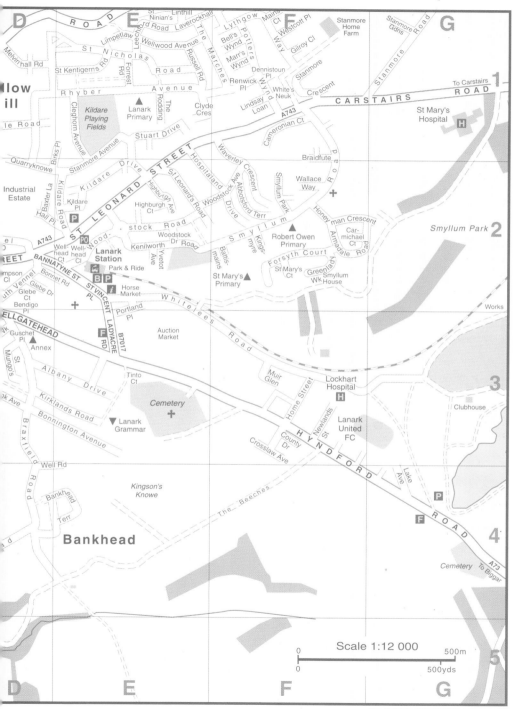

5

D

ROAD
Melvinhall Rd
le Road
Rhyber
Quarryknowe
Birks Pl
Industrial Estate
Baxter La
Kildare Road
Hall Pl
el
A743
EET
STREET
Thompson Cl
Venner Dr
South
Glebe Dr
Glebe Ct
Bendigo Pl
ELLGATEHEAD
Guschet Pl
St Mungo's
k Ave
Braxfield Road
d
Well Rd
Bankhead Terr

E

Limpetlaw
St Nicholas Rd
St Kentigerns Rd
Forrest Rd
Cleghorn Avenue
Kildare PL
Kildare Pl
Wellhead Ct
Wellhead Cl
BANNATYNE ST
Bonnet Rd
Albany Drive
Kirklands Road
Bonnington Avenue
Bankhead

St Ninian's
Ford Road
Linthill
Wellwood Avenue
Leechlee Rd
Laverockhall
The Marches
Russell Rd
ROAD
AVENUE
The Rodding
Kildare Playing Fields
Lanark Primary
Stuart Drive
Stanmore Avenue
Kildare Drive
ST LEONARD
Highburgh Ave
Highburgh Ct
Woodstock Road
Kenilworth
Woodstock
Dr
Lanark Station
Park & Ride
ST VINCENT PL
LADYACRE RD
B7017
Portland Pl
Horse Market
Auction Market
Tinto Ct
Cemetery
Lanark Grammar
Kingson's Knowe

F

Lythgow
Mains Ct
Bell's Wynd
Potters Pl
Westcott Pl
Gilroy Cl
Marr's Wynd
Wynd
Dennistoun Pl
Stanmore
Renwick Pl
White's Neuk
Crescent
Lindsay Loan
A743
Cameronian Ct
Waverley Crescent
Hospitaland Drive
St Leonard's Road
Woodstock Ave
Abbotsford Terr
Smyllum Park
Wallace Way
Braidfute
Honeyman Crescent
Smyllum
Robert Owen Primary
Kings myre
Baltis-mains
Forsyth Court
St Mary's Ct
Green Wk
Carmichael Ct
Armadale Road
Smyllum House
St Mary's Primary
Whitelees Road
Muir Glen
Home Street
Lockhart Hospital
Newlands
Lanark United FC
County Dr
Crosslaw Ave
HYNDFORD
The Beeches

G

Stanmore Home Farm
Stanmore Gdns
Stanmore Road

1
To Carstairs
CARSTAIRS ROAD
St Mary's Hospital H

Smyllum Park 2

Works

3
Clubhouse

4
Cemetery
A73
To Biggar

Lanark Grammar ▼

Scale 1:12 000

0 —————— 500m
0 —————— 500yds

5

D   E   F   G

For index to street names see page 38

6 LARKHALL

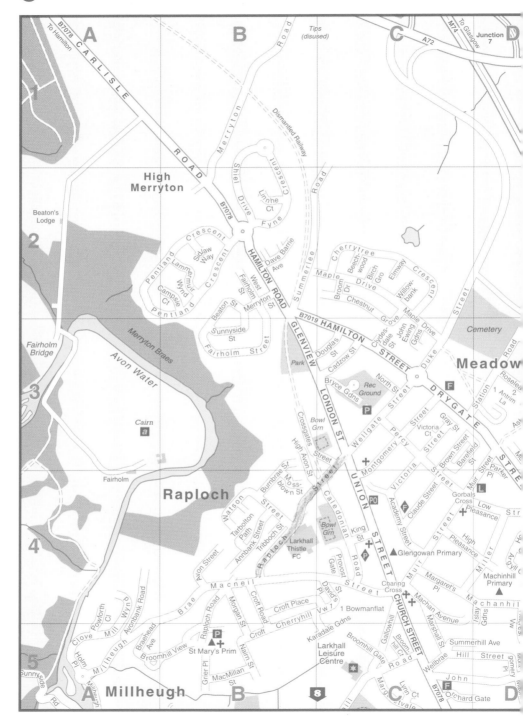

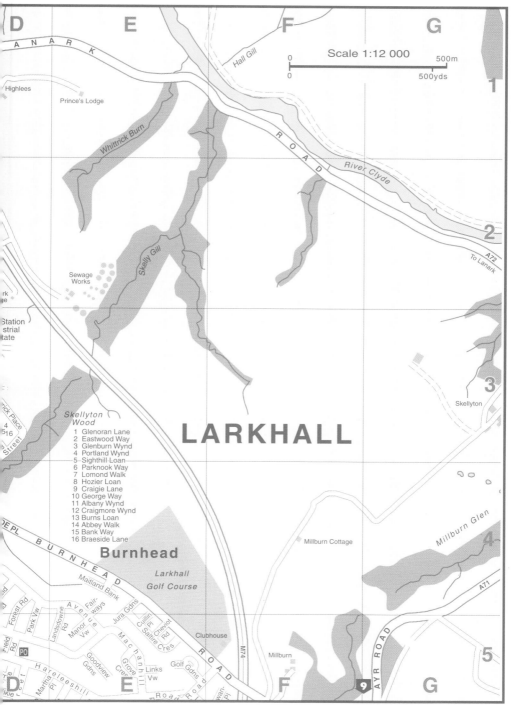

D   **E**   **F**   **G**

Hall Gill

Scale 1:12 000

0   500m
0   500yds

L A N A R K

Highlees

Prince's Lodge

Whittrick Burn

R O A D

River Clyde

1

A72
To Lanark

2

Skelly Gill

Sewage
Works

rk
e

Station
strial
tate

rick Place

4
16

Street

Skellyton

3

*Skellyton
Wood*

1 Glenoran Lane
2 Eastwood Way
3 Glenburn Wynd
4 Portland Wynd
5 Sighthill Loan
6 Parknook Way
7 Lomond Walk
8 Hozier Loan
9 Craigie Lane
10 George Way
11 Albany Wynd
12 Craigmore Wynd
13 Burns Loan
14 Abbey Walk
15 Bank Way
16 Braeside Lane

LARKHALL

Millburn Glen

Millburn Cottage

4

A71

DE PL

B U R N H E A D

Burnhead

Maitland Bank

*Larkhall
Golf Course*

Forest Rd

Park Vw

Landsdowne
Rd

Manor
Vw

Fair-
ways

A v e n u e

Jura Gdns

Cuillin Pl

Saltire Cres

Cheviot
Rd

M a c h a n h i l l

Clubhouse

R O A D

M74

Millburn

A Y R R O A D

R O A D

5

Field
Rd

PO

Martha

Hareleeshill

Goodview
Gdns

Grove
Cres

Links
Vw

Golf Gdns

wart
Pl

9

D   **E**   **F**   **G**

For index to street names see pages 39-40

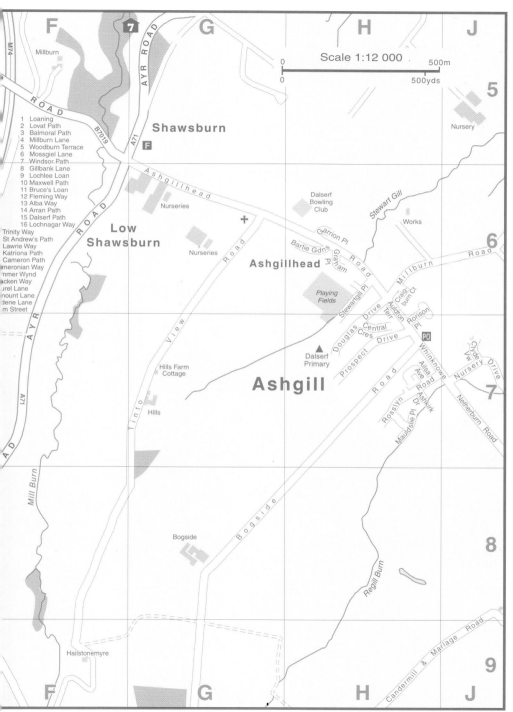

Scale 1:12 000

0   500m

0   500yds

Millburn

M74

ROAD

Shawsburn

AYR ROAD

B7019

A71

F

Low
Shawsburn

ROAD

AYR

A71

AD

Ashgillhead

Nurseries

Nurseries

Ashgillhead

Hills Farm
Cottage

Tinto View

Hills

Mill Burn

Bogside

Bogside

Hailstonemyre

Dalserf
Bowling
Club

Carrion Pl

Bartie Gdns

Graham Pl

Stewart Gill

Works

Road

Millburn

Road

Playing
Fields

Dalserf
Primary

Stewartgill Pl

Douglas Drive

Central
Cres

Prospect Drive

Auldton Terr

Rorison Pl

Craigburn Ct

PO

Whinknowe

Alisa Ave

Road

Rosslyn Dr

Maudslie Pl

Ashkirk Pl

Netherburn Road

Clyde Vw

Nursery Drive

Ashgill

Regill Burn

Candermill & Marlage Road

Nursery

1 Loaning
2 Lovat Path
3 Balmoral Path
4 Millburn Lane
5 Woodburn Terrace
6 Mossgiel Lane
7 Windsor Path
8 Gillbank Lane
9 Lochlee Loan
10 Maxwell Path
11 Bruce's Loan
12 Fleming Way
13 Alba Way
14 Arran Path
15 Dalserf Path
16 Lochnagar Way
Trinity Way
St Andrew's Path
Lawrie Way
Katriona Path
Cameron Path
meronian Way
mmer Wynd
acken Way
urel Lane
nount Lane
dene Lane
m Street

F   G   H   J

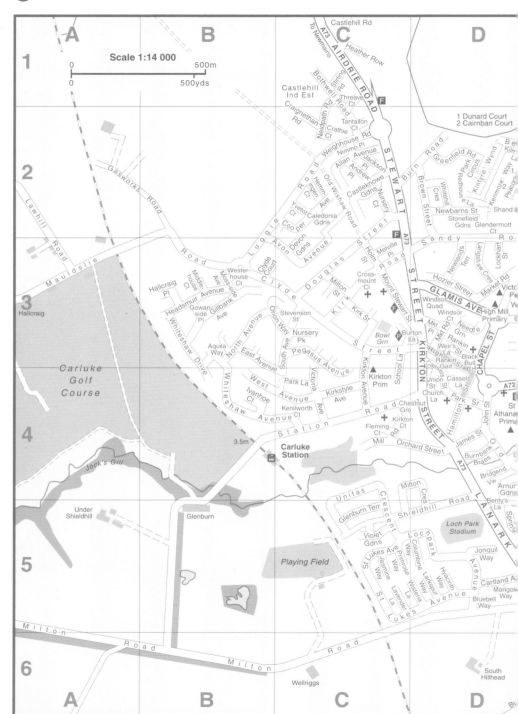

Scale 1:14 000

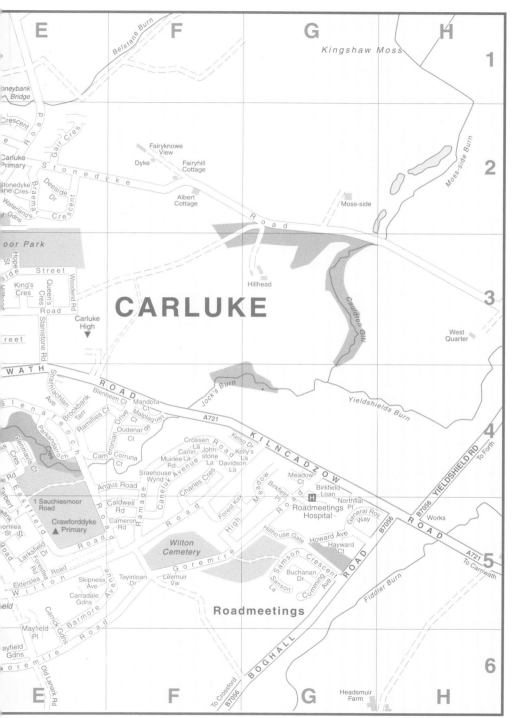

E F G H

1

Kingshaw Moss

Belstane Burn

oneybank
Bridge

Crescent

Moss-side Burn

Carluke
Primary

Gair Cres

Fairyknowe
View

Dyke Fairyhill
Cottage

2

Stonedyke
ine Cres

Deeside
Dr

Braemar

Stonedyke

Albert
Cottage

Moss-side

Waterland's
d Gdns

Cres

Road

oor Park

Hope
St

Street

Hillhead

Cauldron Gill

3

King's
Cres

Queen's
Cres

Woodend Rd

CARLUKE

West
Quarter

reet

Road

Stanistone Rd

Carluke
High
▼

WATH

ROAD

Jock's Burn

A721

Yieldshields Burn

Strathlachan
Ave

Blenheim Ct

Mandora
Ct

Brookbank
Terr

Ramillies Ct

Malplaquet

KILNCADZOW

Glenmavis Ct

Parkandarroch
Cres

Cam
Ct

Drive

Corruna
Ct

Oudenarde
Ct

Crossen
La

Kelso Dr

Carlin
Muirlee
Rd

John-
stone
La

Kelly's
La

Davidson
La

YIELDSHIELD RD

To Forth

Sraehouse
Wynd

Charles Cres

Meadow
Ct

Birkfield
Loan

Northflat
Pl

B7056

Angus Road

Caldwell
Rd

Caneluk Avenue

Forest Kirk

Meadow

Birkfield
Pl

Roadmeetings
Hospital

General Roy
Way

Works

ROAD

A721

To Carnwath

5

Cornlea
St

Larksfield
Dr

Foreslea

Eastfield

Cameron
Rd

Road

High

Hillhouse Gate

Howard Ave

Hayward
Ct

ROAD

Elderslea
Rd

Forestlea
Road

Wilton

Skipness
Ave

Road

Tayinloan
Dr

Leemuir
Vw

Goremire

Samson Crescent

Buchanan
Dr

Cumming Ave

Fiddler Burn

Carradale
Gdns

Barmore
Ave

Samson
La

Mayfield
Pl

Carrick Gdns

Road

Roadmeetings

ield

ayfield
Gdns

oremire

Old Lanark Rd

BOGHALL

To Crossford
B7056

Headsmuir
Farm

6

E F G H

1 Sauchiesmoor
Road

Crawforddyke
▲ Primary

*Wilton
Cemetery*

4

Lesmahagow

Junction 10

Star Truck Stop

Milton Farm

Milton Industrial Estate

Wellburn

Strathaven Road

Dillarsview
Springbank
Wellburn Ave
Oakbank
Muirsland Pl
Gilchrist Loan
Steel Way
Douglas Ave
Gilbert Dr
McKirdy Dr
Greenshields Ct
Cairncross Cres
Craigie Brae
Clannochdyke

Cemetery

Milton Park Sq
Nethan Vale Terr
The Crescent

Strathaven Road

Carlisle Road
4.3m
Milton Bridge
Station Rd
FB Telfords Bridge
The Toll
Monks Bridge
FB

Milton Primary
Lesmahagow High
School Rd
Lesmahagow High
Milton Terr
Milton Pl
Broom Park Dr
Wellwood Rd
Bloomfield Rd
Abbeygreen

Lynallan

North Garngour

Mid Gargour
Garngour

South Gargour

Playing Fields

Greenburn
Whyte Wynd
Mayfield
Elmbank
Beechwood Cres
New Road
Cordiner Rd
Cordiner Ct
Old Crae
Bankhouse Rd
Baker's Brae
Church Sq
Priory (remains)
Bereholm
McKirdy

Glebe Gdns
Langdykeside
Cem
FB
Foxe's Castle

To Blackwood
B7078
M74

14

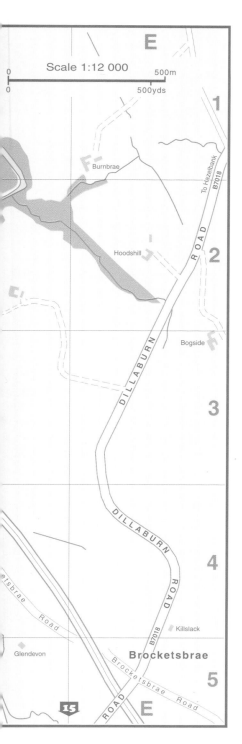

Scale 1:12 000

500m

500yds

Index to Lesmahagow

Abbeygreen Road	14 C6		Oakbank	12 A3
Abbeygreen	12 C4		Old Brae	14 C5
Abbeyhill Crescent	15 D6		Pathfoot Smithy	12 D4
Abbeyhill Road	15 D7		Priory Avenue	14 D5
Abbots Knowe	14 D6		Priory Place	15 D6
Abbots Way	14 D6		Priory Road	15 D6
Auldton Drive	15 D7		School Road	12 C4
Baker's Brae	14 C5		Southview	14 D5
Balgray Road	15 D7		Springbank	12 A3
Bankhead Avenue	15 D6		Station Road	12 C3
Bankhead Road	14 D6		Steel Way	12 B3
Bankhouse Road	14 C5		Strathaven Road	12 A2
Beechwood Crescent	14 B5		Strathaven Road	12 C3
Bereholm	14 C5		Teiglum Road	12 B2
Bloomfield Road	12 C4		Toll, The	12 C4
Bog Road	15 D8		Turfholm	14 C5
Bracken Brae	15 D7		Wellburn Avenue	12 A3
Briar Bank	15 D7		Wellwood Road	12 C4
Brocketsbrae Road	15 E5		Whyte Wynd	14 C5
Broom Park Drive	12 C4		Woodpark	14 D5
Broughden Way	14 D7		Woodside Close	14 C5
Cairncross Crescent	12 B3			
Carlisle Road	12 C3			
Carlisle Road	15 D6			
Church Square	14 C5			
Cordiner Court	14 C5			
Cordiner Road	14 C5			
Craigie Brae	12 B3			
Crescent, The	12 C3			
Differick Drive	14 D7			
Dillarburn Road	13 E3			
Dillarburn Road	13 E4			
Dillarsview	12 A3			
Douglas Avenue	12 B3			
Eastwood Drive	15 D5			
Eastwood Place	15 D6			
Eastwood Road	15 E6			
Elmbank	14 C5			
Fern Dale	15 D7			
Firhill Road	15 D7			
Garngour Road	12 B4			
Gateside Walk	15 D7			
Gilbert Drive	12 B3			
Gilchrist Loan	12 B3			
Glebe Gardens	14 C5			
Greenburn	14 C5			
Greenshields Court	12 B3			
Hillcrest	14 D7			
Kelso Avenue	15 D7			
Langdykeside	14 C5			
McKirdy Drive	12 B3			
Mayfield	14 C5			
Mill Road	14 C5			
Milton	12 C4			
Milton Park Square	12 C3			
Milton Place	12 C4			
Milton Terrace	12 C4			
Monks Knowe	14 D6			
Monks Way	15 D6			
Monks Way	15 D7			
Moss Side	15 D7			
Muirsland Place	12 A3			
Nethan Vale Terrace	12 C3			
New Road	14 C5			
New Trows Road	14 B6			
New Trows Road	14 B7			

14 LESMAHAGOW

North Garngour

12

Mid Gargour

Garngour

South Gargour

Greenburn

Whyte Wynd

Mayfield

Embank

Beechwood Cres

New Road

Road

Bankhouse Rd

Cordiner Rd

Cordiner Ct

Baker's Brae

L

Old Brae

Bereholm

Church Sq
Priory
(remains)

a

Cem

Broom Park

High

Terr
Milton Pl

Wellwood Rd

Bloomfield Rd

Abbeygreen

FB

Playing Fields

Glebe Gdns

Langdykeside

FB

Foxe Cast

PO McKirdy Park

Kilhall Burn

New Trows Road

Turfholm Bridge

Bowl Grn

Mill Rd

Turfholm

Turfholm Ind Est

Woodside Ci

Abbeygreen

Woo Pa

Woodla Park

Auchtykirnal

Birkdale

Birkwood Hospital

H

FB

Abbot's Well

FB

St Bride's Well

Lesmahagow

Letham Mains

Mavis Bank

River Nethan

Ardoch

New Trows

Boughden Braes

Netherhouse

Latham

Road

Woodhead

New Trows

Greystone

Woodhead

New Trows

Th

Scale 1:12 000

0 — 500m
0 — 500yds

A   B   C

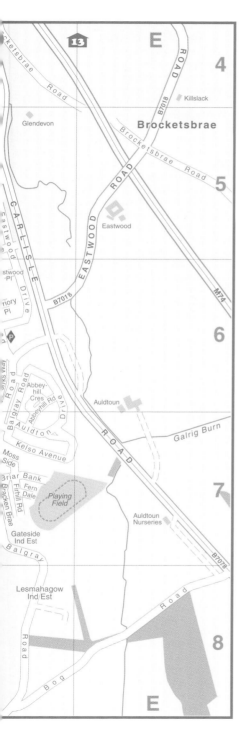

Index to Lesmahagow

Abbeygreen Road	14 C6	Oakbank	12 A3
Abbeygreen	12 C4	Old Brae	14 C5
Abbeyhill Crescent	15 D6	Pathfoot Smithy	12 D4
Abbeyhill Road	15 D7	Priory Avenue	14 D5
Abbots Knowe	14 D6	Priory Place	15 D6
Abbots Way	14 D6	Priory Road	15 D6
Auldton Drive	15 D7	School Road	12 C4
Baker's Brae	14 C5	Southview	14 D5
Balgray Road	15 D7	Springbank	12 A3
Bankhead Avenue	15 D6	Station Road	12 C3
Bankhead Road	14 D6	Steel Way	12 B3
Bankhouse Road	14 C5	Strathaven Road	12 A2
Beechwood Crescent	14 B5	Strathaven Road	12 C3
Bereholm	14 C5	Teiglum Road	12 B2
Bloomfield Road	12 C4	Toll, The	12 C4
Bog Road	15 D8	Turfholm	14 C5
Bracken Brae	15 D7	Wellburn Avenue	12 A3
Briar Bank	15 D7	Wellwood Road	12 C4
Brocketsbrae Road	15 E5	Whyte Wynd	14 C5
Broom Park Drive	12 C4	Woodpark	14 D5
Broughden Way	14 D7	Woodside Close	14 C5
Cairncross Crescent	12 B3		
Carlisle Road	12 C3		
Carlisle Road	15 D6		
Church Square	14 C5		
Cordiner Court	14 C5		
Cordiner Road	14 C5		
Craigie Brae	12 B3		
Crescent, The	12 C3		
Differick Drive	14 D7		
Dillarburn Road	13 E3		
Dillarburn Road	13 E4		
Dillarsview	12 A3		
Douglas Avenue	12 B3		
Eastwood Drive	15 D5		
Eastwood Place	15 D6		
Eastwood Road	15 E6		
Elmbank	14 C5		
Fern Dale	15 D7		
Firhill Road	15 D7		
Garngour Road	12 B4		
Gateside Walk	15 D7		
Gilbert Drive	12 B3		
Gilchrist Loan	12 B3		
Glebe Gardens	14 C5		
Greenburn	14 C5		
Greenshields Court	12 B3		
Hillcrest	14 D7		
Kelso Avenue	15 D7		
Langdykeside	14 C5		
McKirdy Drive	12 B3		
Mayfield	14 C5		
Mill Road	14 C5		
Milton	12 C4		
Milton Park Square	12 C3		
Milton Place	12 C4		
Milton Terrace	12 C4		
Monks Knowe	14 D6		
Monks Way	15 D6		
Monks Way	15 D7		
Moss Side	15 D7		
Muirsland Place	12 A3		
Nethan Vale Terrace	12 C3		
New Road	14 C5		
New Trows Road	14 B6		
New Trows Road	14 B7		

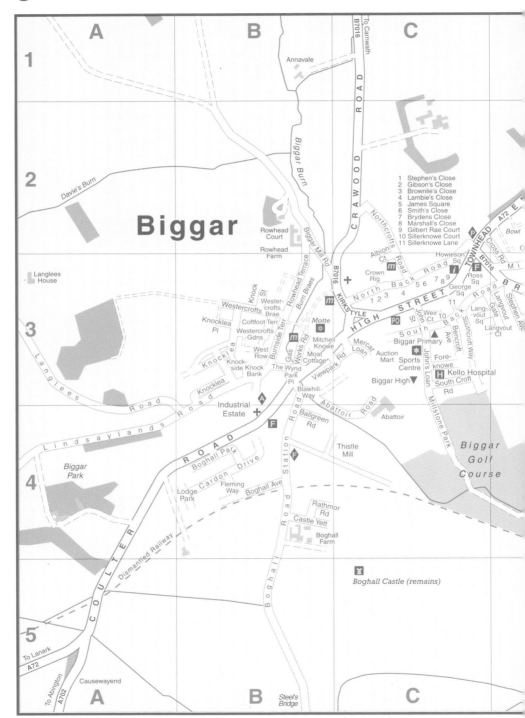

Biggar

1 Stephen's Close
2 Gibson's Close
3 Brownlie's Close
4 Lambie's Close
5 James Square
6 Smith's Close
7 Brydens Close
8 Marshall's Close
9 Gilbert Rae Court
10 Sillerknowe Court
11 Sillerknowe Lane

Annavale

Biggar Burn

To Carnwath
B7016

CRAWOOD ROAD

Davie's Burn

Langlees House

Rowhead Court
Rowhead Farm

Northcrofts Road

Albion's Ct
Crown Rig

Howieson Sq

TOWNHEAD
Cross Rd
B7016

A72 E

Bowl

Ross Sq
George Sq

Biggar Mill Rd
B7016

KIRKSTYLE

North Back Road

HIGH STREET
1 2 3 4 5 6 7 8 9

11

Westercrofts
Knock St
Westercrofts Brae
Coftfoot Terr
Westercrofts Gdns

Rowhead Terrace
Burn Braes

Weir Ct
John St

10

George Sq
Back Road
Langvout Gate
Langvout Sq
Langvout Ct
Stephen Av

Knocklea Pl
Burnside Terr

Motte
West Row

Mitchell Knowe
Moat Cottages
Viewpark Rd

South
PO
John's Loan

Biggar Primary
Mercat Loan

Bencroft Ave
Southcroft Way

Knockside Knock Bank
Knocklea
The Wynd
Knock Park Pl

Auction Mart
Sports Centre

Fore-knowe
H Kello Hospital
South Croft Rd

Langlees Road

Industrial Estate

Blawhill Way

Biggar High

Abattoir Road
Abattoir

Millstone Park

Lindsaylands Road

Boghall Park
Cardon Drive
Ballgreen Rd

Station Road
Works Rd
Gas

Biggar Golf Course

Biggar Park

Lodge Park
Fleming Way
Boghall Ave

Thistle Mill

Rathmor Rd
Castle Yett
Boghall Farm

COULTER ROAD

Dismantled Railway

Boghall Road

Boghall Castle (remains)

To Lanark
A72

To Abington
A702

Causewayend

Steel's Bridge

Index to Biggar

Abattoir Road	B3	Langlees Road	A3
Albion Court	C3	Langvout Court	D3
Ballgreen Road	B4	Langvout Gate	D3
Bencroft Avenue	C3	Langvout Square	C3
Biggar Mill Road	B2	Leafield Road	D2
Blawhill Way	B3	Lindsaylands Road	A4
Boghall Ave	B4	Lodge Park	B4
Boghall Park	B4	Manse Drive	D3
Boghall Road	D5	Marshall's Close (8)	C3
Bowling Green Lane	D2	Mercat Loan	C3
Broughton Road	D3	Mid Road	D3
Brownlie's Close (3)	C3	Millstone Park	C4
Brydens Close (7)	C3	Mitchell Knowe	B3
Burnside Terrace	B3	Moat Cottage	B3
Cardon Drive	B4	North Back Road	C3
Castle Yett	B4	Northcrofts Road	C2
Coftfoot Terrace	B3	Park Place	B3
Colliehill Road	D3	Park Road	D3
Coulter Road	A5	Rathmor Road	B4
Crawood Road	C2	Ross Square	C3
Cross Road	D2	Rowhead Court	B2
Crown Rig	C3	Rowhead Terrace	B3
Dene Park	D3	Sillerknowe Court (10)	C3
Edinburgh Road	D2	Sillerknowe Lane (11)	C3
Fleming Way	B4	Smith's Close (6)	C3
Foreknowe	C3	South Back Road	C3
Gas Works Road	B3	South Croft Road	C3
George Square	C3	Southcroft Way	C3
Gibson's Close (2)	C3	Springdale Drive	D2
Gilbert Rae Court (9)	C3	Stanehead Park	D3
Guildies Loan	D2	Station Road	B4
High Street	C3	Stephen Avenue	D3
Howieson Square	C3	Stephen's Close (1)	C3
James Square (5)	C3	Sykehead Drive	D3
John Street	C3	Townhead	C3
John's Loan	C3	Viewpark Road	B3
Kirkstyle	C3	Weir Court	C3
Knock Bank	B3	West Row	B3
Knock Street	B3	Westercrofts	B3
Knocklea	B3	Westercrofts Brae	B3
Knocklea Place	B3	Westercrofts Gardens	B3
Knockside	B3	Wynd, The	B3
Lambie's Close (4)	C3		

Scale 1:12 000

0 — 500m

0 — 500yds

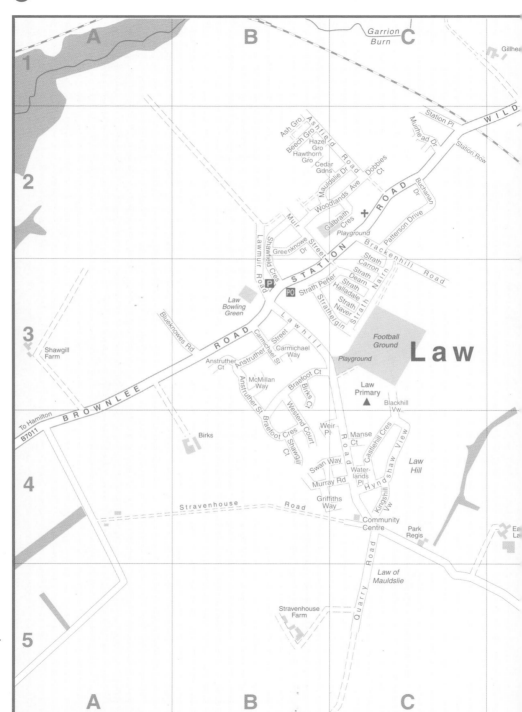

A B C

1

2

Garrion Burn

Gillhea

WILD

Station Pl

Station Row

Muirhead Dr

Ash Gro
Beech Gro
Hazel Gro
Hawthorn Gro
Cedar Gdns

Ashfield Road

Mauldslie Dr

Woodlands Ave

Dobbies Ct

Buchanan Dr

STATION ROAD

Galbraith Cres

Playground

Patterson Drive

Brackenhill Road

Greenknowe Dr

Muir Street

Shawfield Cres

Lawmuir Road

3

Blueknowes Rd

BROWNLEE ROAD

Law Bowling Green

Lawhill Street

Carmichael St

Carmichael Way

Anstruther Ct

Anstruther St

Braefoot Cres

McMillan Way

Birks Ct

Braefoot Ct

Westend Court

Shawgill Ct

Shawgill Farm

Strath Carron
Strath Dearn
Strath Nairn
Strath Halladale
Strath Naver
Strathelgin

Strath Peffer

Football Ground

Playground

Law

Law Primary

Blackhill Vw

Weir Pl

Manse Ct

Castlehill Cres

Hyndshaw View

Law Hill

4

To Hamilton
B7011

BROWNLEE

Birks

Swan Way

Murray Rd

Waterlands Pl

Griffiths Way

Road

Kingshill Vw

Stravenhouse Road

Community Centre

Park Regis

Ea
La

5

Law of Mauldslie

Stravenhouse Farm

Quarry Road

A B C

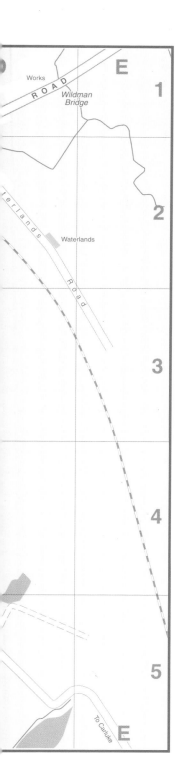

Index to Law

Anstruther Court	B3
Anstruther Street	B3
Ash Grove	B2
Ashfield Road	B2
Beech Grove	B2
Birks Court	B3
Birks Road	A4
Blackhill View	C3
Blueknowes Road	A3
Brackenhill Road	C2
Braefoot Court	B3
Braefoot Crescent	B4
Brownlee Road	A3
Buchanan Drive	C2
Carmichael Street	B3
Carmichael Way	B3
Castlehill Crescent	C4
Cedar Gardens	B2
Dobbies Court	C2
Galbraith Crescent	C2
Greenknowe Drive	B2
Griffiths Way	B4
Hawthorn Grove	B2
Hazel Grove	B2
Hyndshaw View	C4
Kingshill View	C4
Lawhill Road	B3
Lawmuir Road	B2
McMillan Way	B3
Manse Court	C4
Mauldslie Drive	B2
Muir Street	B2
Muirhead Drive	C2
Murray Road	B4
Patterson Drive	C2
Quarry Road	C5
Shawfield Crescent	B2
Shawgill Court	B4
Station Place	C2
Station Road	B3
Station Row	C2
Strath Carron	C3
Strath Dearn	C3
Strath Elgin	B3
Strath Halladale	C3
Strath Nairn	C3
Strath Naver	C3
Strathpeffer	B3
Stravenhouse Road	B4
Swan Way	B4
Waterlands Place	C4
Waterlands Road	D2
Weir Place	B4
Westend Court	B3
Wildman Road	D2
Woodlands Avenue	B2

Scale 1:12 000

0   500m

0   500yds

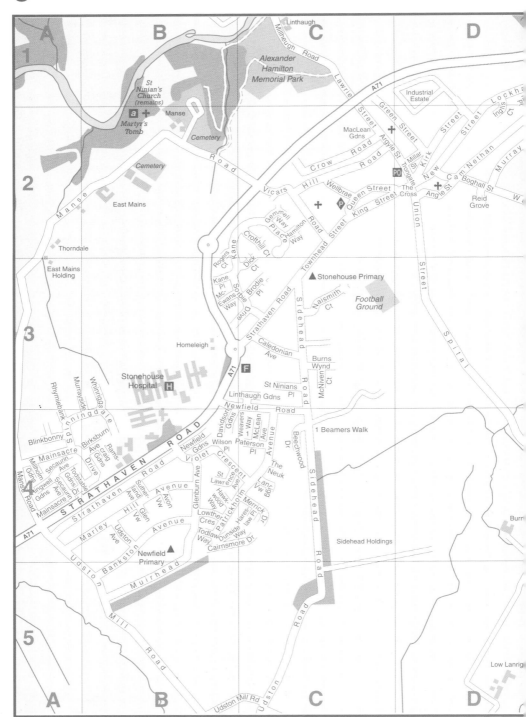

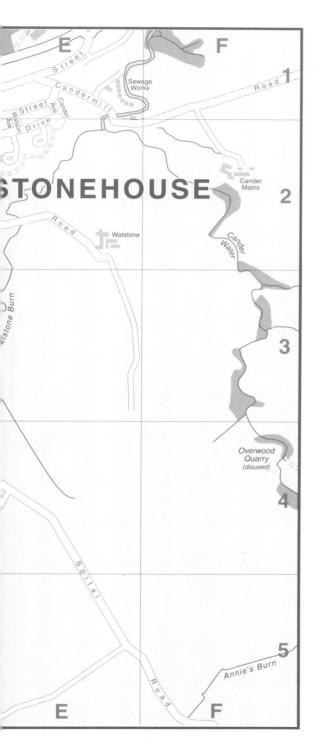

Index to Stonehouse

Angle Street	D2	Manse Road	B2
Argyle Street	C2	Marley Hill Avenue	B4
Avon View	B4	Merrick Drive	C4
Bankston Avenue	B5	Millar Street	D2
Beamers Walk (1)	C4	Millheugh Road	C1
Beechwood Drive	C4	Millholm Gardens	A4
Birksburn Avenue	B4	Muirhead	B5
Blinkbonny	A4	Murray Drive	D2
Boghall Street	D2	Murrayside	A3
Brodie Place	C3	Naismith Court	C3
Burns Wynd	C3	Neuk, The	C4
Cairnsmore Drive	B4	New Street	D2
Caledonian	C3	Newfield Gardens	B4
Avenue		Newfield Road	B3
Cam'Nethan Street	D2	Paterson Place	C4
Cander Avenue	E1	Patrickholm	B4
Candermill Road	E1	Avenue	
Crofthill Court	C2	Queen Street	C2
Cross, The	D2	Ramscraig	B4
Crow Road	C2	Gardens	
Davidson Gardens	B4	Reid Grove	D2
Dick Court	C3	Rhymiebank	A4
Dunside Way	B4	Ringwell Gardens	A4
Gemmell Way	C2	Rogers Court	B2
Glen Avenue	B4	St Ninians Place	C3
Glen Avenue	B4	Secaurin Avenue	A4
Glen View	B4	Sidehead Road	C3
Glenburn Avenue	B4	Sidehead Road	C4
Green Street	C2	Sorbie Drive	B3
Hamilton Way	C2	Spinningdale	A4
Hareslaw Place	C4	Spital Road	D3
Hawkwood Way	B4	Spital Road	F5
Hill Road	C2	Strathaven Road	A4
Inglis Court	D2	Strathaven Road	C3
Kane Place	B3	Sutherland Avenue	B4
Kane Place	B3	Todlaw Way	B4
King Street	C2	Todstable Gardens	A4
Kirk Street	D2	Townhead Street'	C3
Lanrigg View	C4	Trongate	D2
Lawrence Avenue	B4	Udston Avenue	B4
Lawrie Street	C1	Udston Mill Road	B5
Linthaugh Gardens	C3	Udston Road	C5
Lockhart Place	D1	Union Street	D2
Lockhart Street	D1	Vicars Road	C2
Lowther Crescent	B4	Violet Crescent	B4
McEwans Way	B3	Watson Avenue	E2
McLean Avenue	C4	Watstone Road	D2
MacLean Gardens	C2	Weavers Way	C4
McNiven Court	C3	Wellbrae	C2
Mainsacre Drive	A4	Whinriggs	B3
Manse Road	A4	Wilson Place	B4

Scale 1:12 000

0 ———————— 500m

0 ———————— 500yds

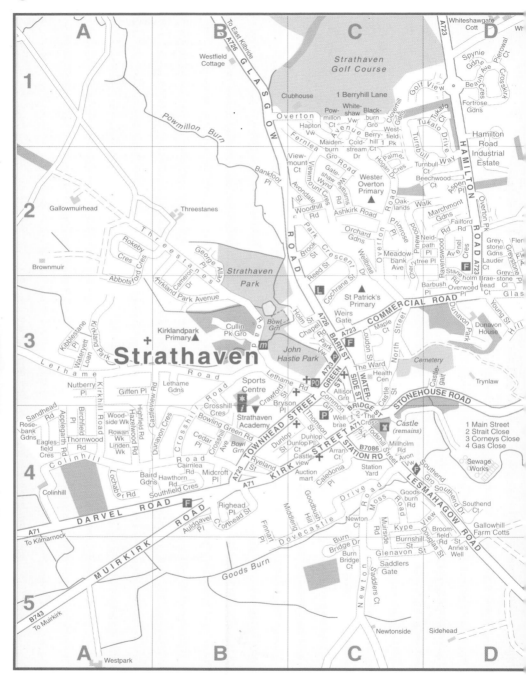

A map of Strathaven showing the following labelled features:

Strathaven Golf Course
Whiteshawgate Cott
Westfield Cottage
Clubhouse
1 Berryhill Lane
Spynie Gdns
Crosskirk
Fortrose Gdns
Powmillon Burn
Overton
Powmillon Ct
Whiteshaw Vw
Blackburn Gro
Golf View
Clovenhill
Tukalo Drive
Hamilton Road Industrial Estate
Fernlea
Hapton Vw
Westfield Pk
Berryhill
Coldstream Ct
Hogan Ct
Palmer Cres
Turnbull Way
Maidenburn Gro
Viewmount Ct
Gateshaw Wynd
Westarns Rd
Turnbull Ct
Beechwood
Aspen Pl
Gallowmuirhead
Threestanes
Avondale St
Viewmount Cres
Wester Overton Primary
Oaklands Walk
Marchmont Gdns
Failford Rd
Woodhill Rd
Ashkirk Road
Primrose
Neidpath Pl
Greystone Gdns
Lauder Rd
Rokeby Cres
George Allan Dr
Cameron Dr
Strathaven Park
Park Crescent
Brook St
Orchard Gdns
Pinewood
Ravenswood
Stoneholm Gdns
Braestone head Ct
Overwood
Brownmuir
Abbotsford Cres
Kirkland Park Avenue
Reed St
Wellbrae
Meadowbank Ave
Barbush Pl
Kibblestane
Watervett Loan
Kirkland Park
Lethame Road
Cullin Pk Gro
Kirklandpark Primary
Holm St
Bowl Grn
Cochrane St
St Patrick's Primary
Maple Ct
Dunavon Park
Dunavon House
Strathaven
Chapel St
Weirs Gate
North St
Cemetery
Trynlaw
John Hastie Park
Park Rd
Loudon St
The Ward
Health Cen
Nutberry Pl
Giffen Pl
Lethame Gdns
Sports Centre
Crawford St
Bryson St
Allison Grn
Common Rd
Castle St
Stonehouse Road
Sandhead
Rosebank Gdns
Birchfield Pl
Woodside Wk
Highfield Rd
Hazelwood Rd
Crosshill Cres
Strathaven Academy
Thomson St
Wellbrae
Castle (remains)
1 Main Street
2 Strait Close
3 Corneys Close
4 Gas Close
Eaglesfield Cres
Applegarth Rd
Thornwood
Rowan Wk
Linden Wk
Cedar Pl
Dunlop Pl
Castleview Ct
Arran Ct
Sewage Works
Colinhill
Lochaber Rd
Baird Gdns
Hawthorn Rd
Midcroft Pl
Cairnlea Rd
Ryeland St
Auction mart
Caledonia Pl
Station Yard
Millholm Rd
Avon
Southend Gro
Southend Ct
Southend
Colinhill
Southfield Cres
Darvel Road
Righead Pl
Auldgavel Pl
Corhead St
Goodbush Hill
Dovecastle Drive
Newton Rd
Murside Rd
Goodsburn Rd
Kype Rd
View
Broomfield Rd
Douglas St
Anne's Well
Gallowhill Farm Cotts
Westpark
Muirkirk Road
Finnart
Middley
Burn Bridge Dr
Burn Bridge Ct
Glenavon St
Burnshill Rd
Saddlers Gate
Saddlers Ct
Sidehead
Goods Burn
To Kilmarnock
To Muirkirk
Newton
Newtonside

Index to Strathaven

Abbotsford Crescent	A3	Eaglesfield Crescent	A4	Overton Park	D2
Allison Green	C3	Failford Road	D2	Overton Road	C3
Applegarth Road	A4	Fernlea Road	C1	Overwood Place	D3
Arran Court	C4	Finnart Place	B4	Palmer Crescent	C2
Ashkirk Road	C2	Flemington Avenue	D2	Park Crescent	C2
Aspen Place	D2	Flemington Place	D2	Park View	C3
Auldgavel Place	B4	Fortrose Gardens	D1	Pierowal Court	D1
Avenel Crescent	D2	Gallowhill Farm Cotts	D4	Pinewood Walk	C2
Avon View	C4	Gas Close (4)	C4	Powmillon Court	C1
Avondale Street	C2	Gateshaw Wynd	C2	Primrose Place	C2
Baird Gardens	A4	George Allan Place	B2	Ravenswood Road	D2
Bankfoot Place	B2	Giffen Place	A3	Reed Street	C2
Barbush Place	D3	Glasgow Road	B1	Righead Place	B4
Barn Street	C3	Glassford Road	D3	Rokeby Crescent	A2
Beauly Avenue	D1	Glenavon Street	C5	Rosebank Gardens	A4
Beechwood Court	D2	Golf View	C1	Rowan Walk	A4
Berryhill Court	C1	Goodbush Hill	C4	Ryeland Street	B4
Berryhill Lane (1)	C1	Goodsburn Road	C4	Saddlers Court	C5
Birchfield Place	A4	Green Street	C3	Saddlers Gate	C5
Blackburn Grove	C1	Greystone Close	D3	Sandhead Road	A4
Bowling Green Road	B4	Greystone Gardens	D2	Southend Court	D4
Braehead Court	D3	Greystone Place	D2	Southend Drive	D4
Bridge Street	C4	Hamilton Road	D2	Southend Grove	D4
Brook Street	C2	Hapton View	C1	Southfield Crescent	B4
Broomfield Road	D4	Hawthorn Road	B4	Springfield Place	D2
Bryson Place	B4	Hazelwood Road	A4	Spynie Gardens	D1
Burn Bridge Court	C5	Highfield Road	A4	St Anne's Well	D5
Burn Bridge Drive	C5	Hills Road	D3	Staneholm Road	D2
Burnshill Street	C5	Hogan Drive	C2	Station Road	C4
Cairnlea Road	B4	Holm Street	C3	Stonehouse Road	D3
Caledonia Place	C4	Kibblestane Place	A3	Strait Close (2)	C4
Cameron Drive	B3	Kirk Street	B4	Thomson Street	C4
Castle Street	C3	Kirkhill Road	A3	Thornwood Road	A4
Castle View	C3	Kirkland Park Avenue	B2	Threestanes Road	B2
Castlegait	D3	Kirkland Park	A3	Todshill Street	C4
Castleview Road	A4	Kype View	C4	Townhead Street	B4
Cedar Place	B4	Lauder Court	D2	Tukalo Court	D1
Chapel Road	C3	Lesmahagow Road	D4	Tukalo Drive	D1
Cherrytree Place	C2	Lethame Gardens	B3	Turnbull Court	D2
Cloverhill Gardens	C1	Lethame Road	A3	Turnbull Way	D2
Cochrane Street	C3	Linden Walk	A4	Viewmount Court	C2
Coldstream Drive	C1	Lochaber Road	A4	Viewmount Crescent	C2
Colinhill Road	A4	Loudon Street	C3	Ward, The	C3
Commercial Road	C3	Maidenburn Grove	C1	Waterside Street	C3
Common Green	C3	Main Street (1)	C4	Wateryett Loan	A3
Corneys Close (3)	C4	Maple Court	C3	Weirs Gate	C3
Crawford Street	B3	Marchmont Gardens	D2	Wellbrae Drive	C2
Crofthead Street	B4	Meadowbank Avenue	C2	Wellbrae	C4
Cross, The	C4	Midcroft Place	B4	Westbarns Road	C2
Crosshill Avenue	B4	Middlerig	C4	Westfield Park	C1
Crosshill Crescent	B4	Millholm Road	C4	Whiteshaw View	C1
Crosshill Road	B4	Moss Road	C4	Woodhill Road	C2
Crosskirk Crescent	D1	Muirkirk Road	A5	Woodside Walk	A4
Cullin Park Grove	B3	Muirside Road	C4	Young Street	D3
Darvel Road	A4	Neidpath Place	D2		
Douglas Street	D5	Newton Court	C4		
Dovecastle Drive	C4	Newton Road	C5		
Dunavon Crescent	B4	North Street	C3		
Dunavon Park	D3	Nutberry Place	A3		
Dunlop Court	C4	Oaklands	C2		
Dunlop Place	C4	Orchard Gardens	C2		
Dunlop Street	B4	Overton Avenue	C1		

Scale 1:14 000

0   500m

0   500yds

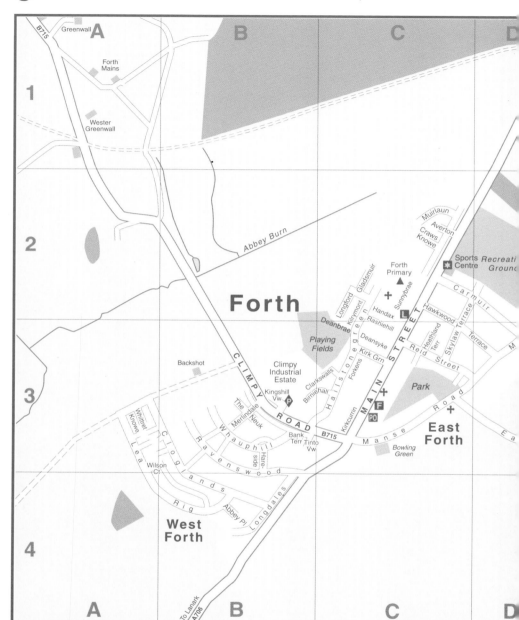

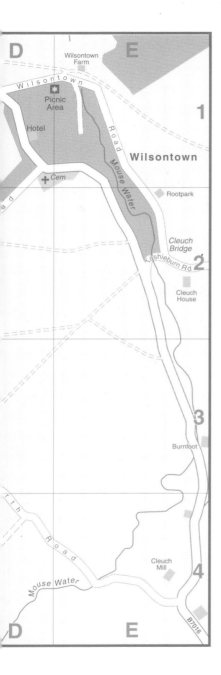

Index to Forth

Abbey Place	B4
Averton	C2
Bank Terrace	B3
Birniehall	B3
Carmuir	C2
Clarkswalls	C3
Climpy Road	B3
Cloglands	B3
Crawsknowe	C2
Deanbrae	C3
Deansyke	C3
East Forth Road	D3
Forkens	C3
Gladmuir	C2
Hailstone Green	C3
Handax	C2
Hareside	B3
Hawkwood Terrace	C2
Heathland Terrace	C3
Kilrymont	C2
Kingshill View	B3
Kircurrin	C3
Kirk Green	C3
Lea Rig	A3
Longdales	B4
Longford	C2
Main Street	C3
Manse Road	C3
Merlindale	B3
Muirlaun	C2
Neuk, The	B3
Rashiehill	C2
Ravenswood	B3
Reid Street	C3
Skylaw Terrace	C3
Sunnybrae	C2
Tashieburn Road	E2
Tinto View	B3
Whauphill	B3
Whittret Knowe	A3
Wilson Court	A3
Wilsontown Road	E1

Scale 1:12 000

0   500m

0   500yds

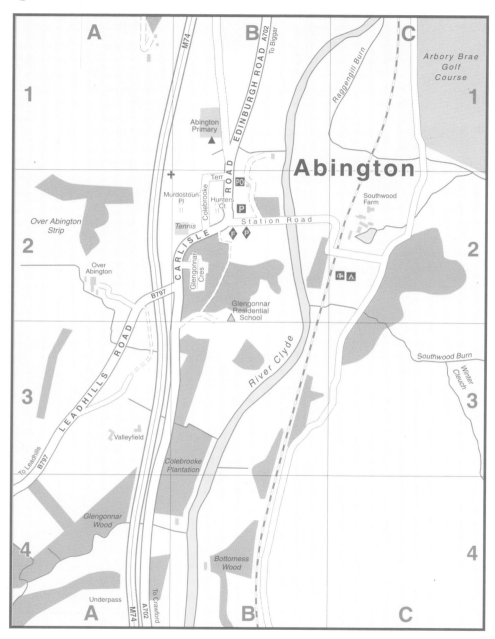

Abington

Arbory Brae Golf Course

Abington Primary

Raggengill Burn

Southwood Farm

Over Abington Strip

Over Abington

Murdostoun Pl

Colebrooke Terr

Hunters Ct

Station Road

Tennis

Glengonnar Cres

Glengonnar Residential School

River Clyde

Southwood Burn

Winter Cleuch

Valleyfield

Colebrooke Plantation

Glengonnar Wood

Bottomess Wood

Underpass

To Leadhills

To Crawford

To Biggar

EDINBURGH ROAD

CARLISLE ROAD

LEADHILLS ROAD

B797

A702

M74

Index to Abington

Carlisle Road	B2	Leadhills Road	A3
Colebrooke Terrace	B2	Murdostoun Place	B2
Edinburgh Road	B1	Station Road	B2
Glengonnar Crescent	B2		
Hunters Court	B2		

Scale 1:12 000

0   500m

0   500yds

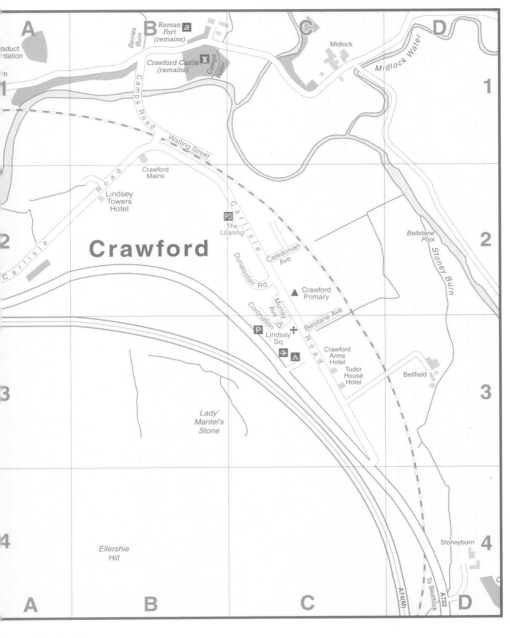

Crawford

dex to Crawford

stane Avenue	C3	Dunalastair Road	C2
ledonian Avenue	C2	Lindsay Square	C3
mps Road	B1	Loaning, The	C2
rlisle Road	A2, C2	Murray Avenue	C2
ronation Drive	C3	Watling Street	B1

Scale 1:12 000

0   500m

0   500yds

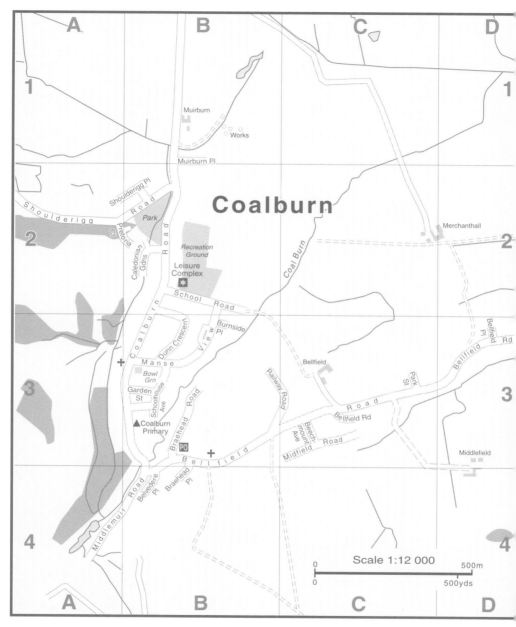

Coalburn

Index to Coalburn

	Braehead Road	B3	Middlemuir Road	A4	Schoolhouse Avenue	B
	Burnside place	B3	Midfield Road	C3	Shoulderigg Place	B
Beechmount Avenue	C3	Caledonian Gardens	B2	Muirburn Place	B1	Shoulderigg Road	A
Bellfield Place	D3	Coalburn Road	B3	Park Street	C3		
Bellfield Road	B3	Dunn Crescent	B3	Pretoria Court	A2		
Belvedere Place	B4	Garden Street	B3	Railway Road	B3		
Braehead Place	B4	Manse view	B3	School Road	B2		

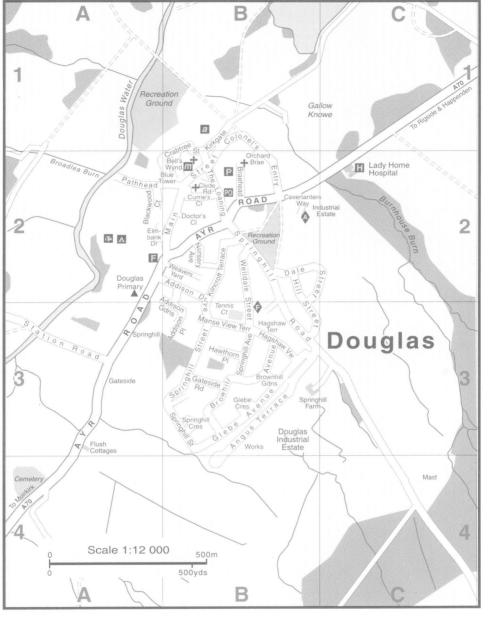

Douglas

Scale 1:12 000

Index to Douglas

Addison Drive	B2	Braehead	B2	Currie's Close	B2
Addison Gardens	B2	Browhill Avenue	B3	Dale Street	B2
Addison Place	B3	Brownhill	B3	Doctor's Close	B2
Angus Terrace	B3	Gardens (1)		Elmbank Drive	A2
Ayr Road	A3	Brownhill		Gateside Road	B3
Bell's Wynd	B2	Clyde Road	B2	Glebe Avenue	B3
Blackwood Court	A2	Colonel's Entry	B1	Glebe Crescent	B3
Blue Tower	A2	Covenanters Way	B2	Hagshaw Terrace	B3
		Crabtree Street	B1	Hagshaw View	B3
				Hawthorn Place	B3

Hill Street	B2	Springhill Avenue	B3
Kilncroft Terrace	B2	Springhill Crescent	B3
Kirkgate	B1	Springhill Road	B2
Loaning, The	B2	Springhill Street	B3
Main Street	B2	Springhill View	B3
Manse View	B3	Station Road	A3
Terrace		Weavers Yard	B2
Nursery Avenue	B2	Welldale Street	B2
Orchard Brae	B2		
Pathhead	A2		

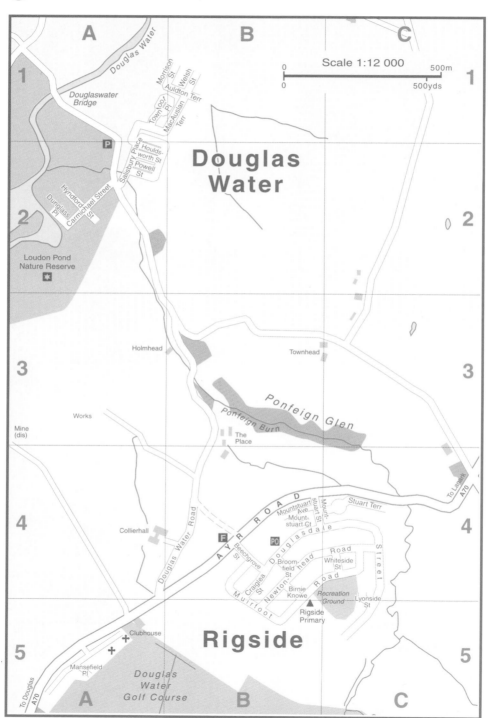

Scale 1:12 000

Douglas Water

Rigside

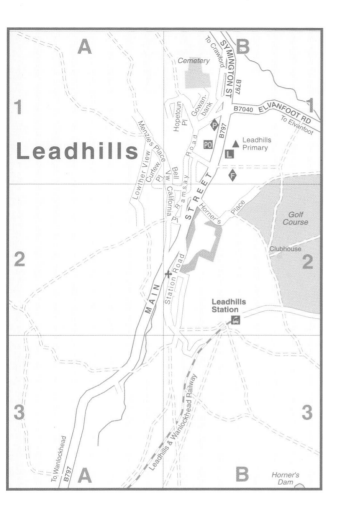

Leadhills

Scale 1:12 000

0   500m

0   500yds

Index to Douglas Water

Auldton Terrace	B1
Carmichael Street	A2
Dunglass Place	A2
Houldsworth Street	A2
Hyndford Street	A2
MacAuslan Terrace	B1
Morrison Street	A1
Powell Street	A2
Salisbury Place	A2
Townfoot Place	A1
Welsh Street	B1

Index to Rigside

Ayr Road	B4
Beechgrove Street	B4
Birnie Knowe	B4
Broomfield Street	B4
Craiglea Street	B4
Douglasdale Street	C4
Douglas Water Road	B4
Lyonside Street	C4
Mansefield Place	A5
Mountstuart Avenue	B4
Mountstuart Court	B4
Mountstuart Street	B4
Muirfoot Road	B5
Newtonhead Road	B4
Stuart Terrace	C4
Whiteside Street	C4

Index to Leadhills

Bell View	B1
California Place	B2
Curfew Place	A1
Elvanfoot Road	B1
Gowanbank	B1
Hopetoun Place	B1
Horner's Place	B2
Lowther View	A2
Main Street	A2
Menzies Place	A1
Ramsay Road	B2
Station Road	B2
Symington Street	B1

Scale 1:12 000

0 — 500m
0 — 500yds

Index to Glassford

Alston Street	B2
Avon Crescent	B1
Calder Crescent	B1
Druid Street	B1
Feu Road	A1
Greenbank Crescent	B2
Hunterlees Road	B2
Jackson Street	B1
Jackson Street	B2
Kirkstyle Place	B1
Lang Court (1)	B1
Larkhall Road	B1
Millar Street	A2
Mossknowe Walk	B1
Muirburn Place	B1
Station Road	A1
Townhead Street	A1
Weavers Court	B1
Weavers Lane	B1

Index to Blackwood

Annfield Court	B4
Baird Avenue	A2
Barr Terrace	C4
Baxters Brae	B2
Beeches, The	B1
Beechwood	B3
Braeside Crescent	B3
Braeside Lane	B3
Braesise Terrace	B3
Bruce Terrace	B3
Burns Road	B3
Cairnegie Gardens	A3
Capehall Square (1)	C4
Carlisle Road	C3
Cherry Tree Drive	B2
Craignethan View	B3
Dormiston Place	B3
Dormiston Road	B3
Dukes Walk	C3
Earn Drive	B2
Ellisland Square	C4
Faulds Square	B4
Fleming Gardens	A2
Fraser Drive	B1
Green Ferns	B2
Hawthorndene (2)	C4
Heathfield Drive	B2
Hope Road	C4
Hunters Way	C4
Kingarth Lane	A2
Knoweknack Terrace	B3
Lairs, The	B1
Lanark Road	D3
Lindsey Road	C3
Lochlea	B2
Lochlea Drive	C4
Loganbank Drive	B3
MacAdam Gardens	A2
McKirdy Court	B1
Moffat Court	B1
Morton Court	B1
Napier Gardens	B3
Nethan View	B1
Oak Knowe	B2
Oldham Close	B2
Park Street	C4
Ramsay Gardens	A2
Robertson Close	B4
Rogerhill Close	B3
Rogerhill Drive	A3
Rogerhill Gait	B3
Scott Street	B4
Southfield Close	B3
Southfield Road	B2
Southfield Terrace	C1
Spire View	C4
Strathaven Road	A4
Swan Street	B4
Sycamore Gardens	B1
Thornton Drive	B3
Thornton Road	B3
Treefield Park	C3
Turnpike Road	B2
Vere Road	C3
Vere Road	
Vere Terrace	C4
Violet Bank	C3
Wallace Place	A2
West End Gardens	B1
Westburn Terrace	
Whinny, The	B3
Woodlea	

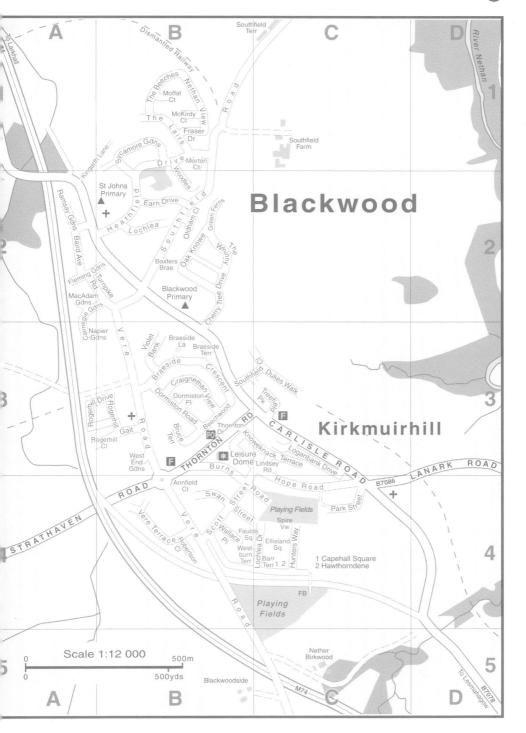

33

Blackwood

Kirkmuirhill

Scale 1:12 000

0 — 500m
0 — 500yds

1 Capehall Square
2 Hawthorndene

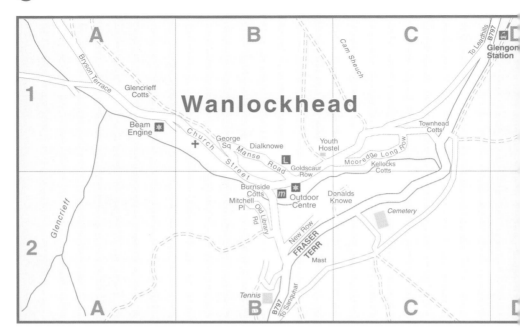

Scale 1:12 000

0 — 500m

0 — 500yds

Index to Wanlockhead

Bryson Terrace A1
Burnside Cottages B2
Church Street B1
Dialknowe B1
Donalds Knowe C2
Fraser Terrace B2
George Square B1
Glencrieff Cottages A1
Goldscaur Row B2
Kellocks Cottages C1
Mitchell Place B2
Manse Road B1
Mooredge Long Row C1
New Row B2
Old Library Road B2
Townhead Cottages C1

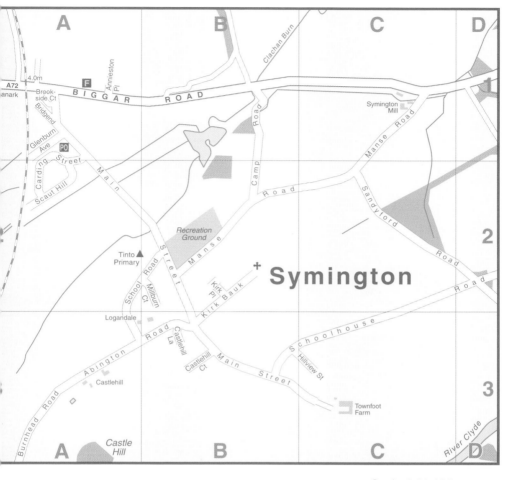

Scale 1:12 000

0   500m

0   500yds

Index to Symington

Abington Road	A3
Annieston Place	A1
Biggar Road	A1
Bridgend	A1
Brookside Court	A1
Burnhead Road	A3
Camp Road	B2
Carding Street	A2
Castlehill Court	B3
Castlehill Lane	B3
Glenburn Avenue	A1
Hillview Street	C3
Kirk Bauk	B3
Kirk Place	B2
Main Street	A2
Main Street	B3
Manse Road	B2
Manse Road	C1
Millburn Court	B2
Sandyford Road	C2
Scaut Hill	A2
School Road	A2
Schoolhouse Road	B3

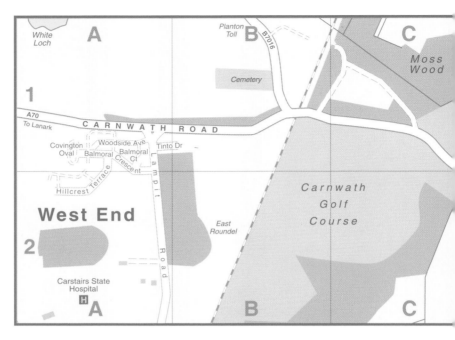

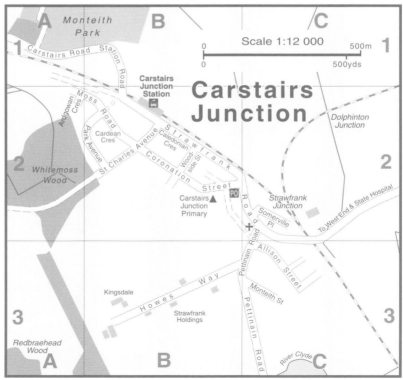

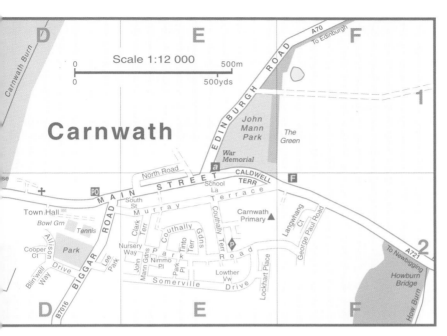

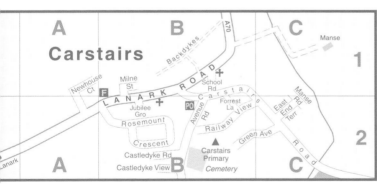

ex to Carnwath

on Drive	D2
noral Court	A1
noral Crescent	A1
ar Road	D2
well Way	D2
dwell Terrace	E1
nwath Road	A1
k Terrace	E2
per Court	D2
thally Gardens	E2
thally Terrace	E2
ington Oval	A1
burgh Road	E1
rge Paul Road	F2
rest Terrace	A2

John Mann Gardens	E2
Lampit Road	A1
Langwhang Court	F2
Lee Park	D2
Lockhart Place	E2
Lowther View	E2
Main Street	E2
Murray Terrace	E2
Nimmo Place	E2
North Road	E2
Nursery Way	E2
Park Place	E2
Park Road	E2
School Lane	E2
Somerville Drive	E2
South Street	E2
Tinto Drive	A1

Tinto Terrace	E2
Woodside Avenue	A1

Index to Carstairs Junction

Allison Street	C3
Ardgowan Crescent	A2
Caledonian Crescent	B2
Cardean Cresecent	B2
Carstairs Road	A1
Coronation Street	B2
Howes Way	B3
Monteith Street	C3
Moss Road	A2

Park Avenue	B2
Pettinain Road	C3
St Charles Avenue	B2
Somerville Place	C2
Station Road	B1
Strawfrank Road	B2
Woodside Street	B2

Index to Carstairs

Avenue Road	B2
Backdykes	B1
Carstairs Road	B1
Castledyke Road	B2
Castledyke View	B2

East End Terr	C2
Forrest Lane	B2
Green Avenue	B2
Jubilee Grove	B2
Lanark Road	B2
Manse Road	C2
Milne Street	B1
Newhouse Court	A1
Railway View	B2
Rosemount Crescent	B2
School Road	B1

Name	Ref	Name	Ref	Name	Ref
Abbotsford Terrace	5 F2	Greyfriars Court	4 D2	Ridgepark Drive	4
Aitken Place	4 D2	Greystone Bauks	4 C2	Ritchie's Close (7)	4
Albany Drive	5 D3	Guschet Place	5 D3	Riverside Road	4
Armadale Road	5 F2	Hall Place	5 D2	Rodding, The	5
Bankhead Terrace	5 E4	Hardacres	4 D1	Rosedale Street	4
Bannatyne Street	5 D2	High Street	4 D2	Russell Road	5
Battismains	5 F2	Highburgh Avenue	5 E2	St Kentigerns Road	5
Baxter Lane	5 D2	Highburgh Court	5 E2	St Leonard Street	5
Beeches, The	5 F4	Hillhouse Farm Road	4 B2	St Leonard's Road	5
Bell's Wynd	5 F1	HillhouseFarm Gate	4 B1	St Mary's Court	5
Bendigo Place	5 D2	Home Street	5 F3	St Mungo's	5
Bernard's Wynd Court	5 D2	Honeyman Crescent	5 F2	St Nicholas Road	5
Birks Place	5 D2	Hope Street	4 D2	St Ninian's	5
Bloomgate	4 D2	Horse Market	5 E2	St Patrick's Court	4
Bonnet Road	5 D2	Hospitaland Drive	5 E2	St Patricks Lane	4
Bonnington Avenue	5 D3	Howacre	4 C1	St Patricks Road	4
Braedale Road	5 D1	Hunter's Close (8)	5 D2	St Vincent Place	5
Braidfute	5 F1	Hyndford Place (3)	4 D2	Scarletmuir	5
Braxfield Road	5 D3	Hyndford Road	5 F3	Shields Loan	4
Braxfield Row	4 C4	Jerviswood Road	4 D2	Shirley's Close (4)	4
Braxfield Terrace	4 C4	Kairnhill Court	4 B2	Silverdale Crescent	4
Brierybank Avenue	5 D3	Kenilworth Road	5 E2	Silverdale Grove	4
Broomgate	4 C3	Kildare Drive	5 E2	Smiddy Court	4
Bull's Close (9)	5 D2	Kildare Place	5 E2	Smyllum House	5
Butts, The	4 C3	Kildare Road	5 E2	Smyllum Park	5
Byretown Road	4 B3	Kingsmyre	5 F2	Smyllum Road	5
Byretown Road	4 B5	Kirkfield Road	4 A3	South Vennel	5
Caithness Row	4 D5	Kirkfieldbank Brae	4 B2	Springfield Gardens	4
Cameronian Court	5 F1	Kirklands Road	5 D3	Staikhill	4
Carmichael Court	5 F2	Ladyacre Road	5 E3	Stanmore Avenue	5
Carstairs Road	5 F1	Lake Avenue	5 G4	Stanmore Crescent	5
Cartland View	4 C1	Lanark Road	4 A1	Stanmore Gardens	5
Castlegate	4 C3	Laverockhall	5 E1	Stanmore Road	5
Chapland Road	4 D1	Leechford Road	5 E1	Stuart Drive	5
Cleghorn Avenue	5 E1	Limpetlaw	5 E1	Sunnyside Road	4
Cleghorn Road	4 D1	Lindsay Loan	5 F1	Thompson Close	5
Clyde Crescent	5 E1	Linthill	5 E1	Tinto Court	5
Clydesholm Court	4 A2	Lockhart Drive	4 B1	West Nemphlar Road	4
County Drive	5 F3	Long Row	4 C4	Wallace Way	5
Cross Key's Close (6)	4 D2	Lythgow Way	5 F1	Waterloo Drive	4
Crosslaw Avenue	5 F3	McKenzies Close (10)	5 D2	Waterloo Road	4
Delves Court	4 D2	Mains Court	5 F1	Waverley Crescent	5
Delves Road	4 D3	Manse Road	4 C2	Weavers Walk	5
Dennistoun Place	5 F1	Marches, The	5 E1	Well Road	5
Double Row	4 C4	Market Court (2)	4 D2	Wellbuttslea Drive	4
Douglas Terrace	4 C2	Market End (1)	4 D2	Wellgate	4
Dovecot Lane	4 D2	Marr's Wynd	5 F1	Wellgatehead	5
Duncan's Close (5)	4 D2	Melvinhall Road	5 D1	Wellhead Close	5
Forrest Road	5 E1	Mousebank Lane	4 C2	Wellhead Court	5
Forsyth Court	5 F2	Mousebank Road	4 C1	Wellington Terrace	4
Friars Grove	4 C2	Mousemill Road	4 A1	Wellwood Avenue	5
Friar's Lane	4 C3	Muir Glen	5 F3	West Port	4
Friar's Park	4 C2	Nemphlat Hill	4 C1	Westcott Place	5
Friar's Wynd	4 C2	New Buildings	4 D4	Wheatland Drive	4
Friarsdene	4 C2	New Lanark Road	4 C4	Wheatlandside	4
Friarsfield	4 C2	Newlands Street	5 F3	Wheatpark Road	4
Friarsfield Road	4 C2	North Vennel	4 D2	Whitehill Crescent	4
Gallowhill Road	5 D2	Nursery Buildings	4 D4	Whitehill Terrace	4
Gilroy Close	5 F1	Nursery Court	4 B2	Whitelees Road	5
Glasgow Road	4 B1	Park Drive	4 B2	White's Neuk	5
Glebe Court	5 D2	Park Place	4 C2	Wide Close	4
Glebe Drive	5 D2	Portland Place	5 E3	Woodstock Road	5
Glebe, The	4 C2	Potters Wynd	5 F1	Woodstock Avenue	5
Grange Court	4 C1	Quarryknowe	5 D2	Woodstock Drive	5
Greenlady Walk	5 F2	Ramoth	4 A2	Yvetot Avenue	5
Greenside Close	4 D2	Renwick Place	5 F1		
Greenside Lane	4 D2	Rhyber Avenue	5 E1		

ey Walk (14)	7 D3	Cander Street	8 D7	Garrion Place	9 H6
otsford Avenue	8 C6	Candermill & Marlage Road	9 H9	George Way (10)	7 D3
demy Street	6 C4	Carlisle Road	6 A1	Gillbank Lane (8)	8 E5
es, The	6 D5	Carlisle Road	8 D7	Glade, The	8 D5
n Street	8 E5	Carrick Place	7 D3	Glen Avenue	8 B7
a Avenue	9 H7	Carrick Street	8 E5	Glen Avenue	8 C6
Way (13)	8 E6	Catrine Street	8 E5	Glen Fruin	8 E6
ny Wynd (11)	7 D3	Central Crescent	9 H7	Glenburn Wynd (3)	6 D3
rt Drive	8 D5	Charing Cross	6 C4	Glengonnar Street	8 C7
way Street	8 E5	Charlotte Path	8 C5	Glenoran Lane (1)	6 D3
bank Street	6 B4	Cherryhill View	6 B4	Glenview	6 B3
im Lane	6 D3	Cherrytree Crescent	6 C2	Golf Gardens	8 E5
ll Gardens	6 D4	Chestnut Grove	6 C2	Goodview Gardens	8 E5
n Path (14)	8 E6	Cheviot Road	8 E5	Gorbals Cross	6 C4
ourn Loan	6 D3	Church Street	6 C4	Graham Place	9 H6
gillhead Road	8 G6	Claude Street	6 C4	Gray Street	6 C3
kirk Drive	9 H7	Clem Attlee Gardens	8 D5	Greenloan View (1)	8 D6
oll Way	8 E6	Clove Mill Wynd	8 E6	Grier Place	6 B5
ston Terrace	9 H6	Clyde View	9 J7	Grove Crescent	7 E5
n Place	8 D8	Clydesdale Street	6 C3	Hamilton Road	6 B2
n Road	8 C7	Coronation Avenue	8 C7	Hamilton Street	6 C3
n Street	6 B4	Coronation Crescent	8 C7	Hareleeshill Road	8 D5
nbank Road	6 A5	Coronation Place (2)	8 C7	Hawick Crescent	8 C6
Road	9 F8	Corrie Way	8 D5	Hawthorn Gardens	8 E5
Road	9 G5	Cosy Neuk	8 E6	Hazeldene Lane (27)	8 E6
d Avenue	8 D7	Covenant Crescent	8 D5	Heath Road	7 D4
our Wynd	8 D6	Craig Burn Court	9 H6	Helen Wynd	8 C5
noral Path (3)	8 E5	Craigbank Road	8 C7	High Avon Street	6 B3
k Way (15)	7 D3	Craigbank Street	8 C6	High Pleasance	6 C4
nockburn Drive	8 E6	Craigie Lane (9)	7 D3	Highfield Road	7 D4
efield Street	6 C3	Craigmore Wynd (12)	7 D3	Hill Street	8 C5
ie Gardens	9 H6	Croft Place	6 B4	Hillcrest View	6 D4
ton Street	6 B2	Croft Road	6 B4	Hillview Crescent	8 D6
ch Avenue	8 F5	Croft	6 B5	Hindsland Road	8 D6
ch Terrace	8 D6	Crossgates Street	6 B3	Holm Place	6 A5
chwood	6 C2	Cuillin Place	8 E5	Hope Crescent	6 D4
ersyde Place	8 C6	Daer Walk	8 C7	Howard Street	8 E6
ram Street (28)	8 E6	Dalserf Path (15)	8 E6	Howie Street	8 D6
h Grove	6 C2	Dave Barrie Avenue	6 B2	Hozier Loan (8)	6 D3
s Road	8 D8	Dee Path	8 C7	Islay Gardens	6 D4
Atholl Drive	8 E6	Dickson Street	8 E6	Jane Court	8 C5
side Road	9 G8	Don Path	8 C7	John Ewing Gardens	6 C3
and Drive	8 D7	Donaldson Road	8 E6	John Place	8 D8
rmanflat (1)	6 C4	Doon Street	8 E5	John Street	8 C5
cken Way (24)	8 E6	Douglas Drive	9 H7	Jura Gardens	8 E5
head Avenue	6 A5	Douglas Street	6 C3	Karadale Gardens	6 C5
eside Lane (16)	7 D3	Drygate Street	6 C3	Katriona Path (20)	8 E6
eside Way (2)	8 D6	Duke Street	6 C3	Keir Hardie Road	8 D6
om Drive	6 C2	Duncan Graham Street	7 D3	Kenshaw Avenue	8 C7
omfield Road	8 D7	Duneaton Wynd	8 D7	Kenshaw Place	8 C7
omhill Court	8 C5	Dunedin Road	8 D6	King Street	6 C4
omhill Gate	6 C5	Earn Gardens	8 C7	Lammer Wynd (23)	8 E6
omhill Road	8 E5	East Machan Street	8 D6	Lammermuir Wynd	6 B2
omhill View	6 A5	Eastwood Way (2)	6 D3	Lanark Road	6 D1
wn Street	6 C3	Elmbank Drive	8 E6	Landsdowne Road	8 E5
ce's Loan (11)	8 E6	Elmway	6 C2	Lansbury Terrace	8 E6
ce Gardens	6 C3	Fairholm Street	6 B3	Laurel Drive	8 E5
nbrae Street	6 B4	Fairways	7 E4	Laurel Lane (25)	8 E6
nhead Road	7 D4	Ferndale	6 C6	Lawrie Way (19)	8 E6
nhead Road	8 E5	Field Road	8 D5	Links View	8 E5
ns Loan (13)	7 D3	Fir Bank Avenue	8 D6	Linnhe Court	6 B2
nside Place	7 D4	Fisher Street	8 D6	Livingstone Gardens	7 D4
zow Street	6 C3	Fleming Way (12)	8 E6	Loan Lea Crescent	8 D6
edonian Road	6 C4	Forest Road	8 D5	Loaning (1)	8 E5
neron Path (21)	8 E6	Forth Place	8 D7	Loch Park Place	8 C6
neronian Way (22)	8 E6	Fyne Crescent	6 B2	Lochlee Loan (9)	8 E5
npsie Court	6 B2	Gallowhill	8 C5	Lochnagar Way (16)	8 E6

INDEX TO LARKHALL

nd Walk (7)	6 D3	Provost Gate	6 C4	Windsor Path (7)	
...on Street	6 C3	Pyatshaw Road	8 D6	Woodburn Terrace (5)	
Lovat Path (2)	8 E5	Quarry Road	8 C5	Woodend Lane	
Low Pleasance	6 D4	Quarry Street	8 D6	Woodland Terrace	
Lynn Court	8 C5	Queensdale Avenue (1)	8 D7	Woodview Road	
Machan Avenue	6 C4	Queensdale Road	8 D7		
Machan Road	8 C5	Rannoch Terrace	8 E6		
Machanhill View	8 D5	Raploch Road	6 B5		
Machanhill	6 D4	Raploch Street	6 B4		
Machanhill	7 E5	Redholme Path (3)	8 D6		
MacMillan Street	6 B5	Riverside Road	8 C7		
MacNeil Street	6 B4	Robert Smillie Crescent	8 D6		
Maitland Bank	7 E4	Rorison Place	9 H7		
Manor View	8 E5	Roselea Street	6 D3		
Manseview	8 D5	Rosemount Lane (26)	8 E6		
Maple Drive	6 C2	Rosslyn Road	9 H7		
Margaret's Place	6 C4	Rowantree Place	9 F5		
Margaretvale Drive	8 C5	Saltire Crescent	8 E5		
Marshall Street	6 C4	Scotia Crescent	8 D6		
Martha Place	8 D5	Scott Street	8 D5		
Mason Street	8 E6	Shaw Street	8 D7		
Mathew McWhirter Place	6 D3	Shawrigg Road	8 E5		
Mauldslie Place	9 H7	Shaw's Road	8 D8		
Maxwell Path (10)	8 E5	Shaw's Road	8 E7		
McCallum Road	8 D6	Shiel Drive	6 B2		
Meadowhill Street	7 D4	Sidlaw Way	6 B2		
Meadows Avenue	7 D4	Sighthill Loan (5)	6 D3		
Melrose Place	8 C6	Skellyton Crescent	8 D6		
Merryton Road	6 B1	Solar Court	8 D7		
Merryton Street	6 B2	Spey Wynd	8 C7		
Middleton Avenue	8 D7	St Andrew's Path (18)	8 E6		
Millburn Lane (4)	8 E5	St David's Place	6 C4		
Millburn Place (3)	8 D7	Station Road	6 D3		
Millburn Road	9 H6	Stewartgill Place	9 H6		
Miller Street	6 D4	Struther & Swinhill Road	8 E8		
Millheugh Brae	6 A5	Struther Street	8 D7		
Millheugh Road	6 A5	Stuart Drive	8 E6		
Millheugh	6 A5	Summerhill Avenue	8 C5		
Montgomery Place	8 D5	Summerlee Road	6 B2		
Montgomery Street	6 C3	Sunnyside Road	6 A5		
Morgan Street	6 B4	Sunnyside Street	6 B3		
Morris Street	8 E6	Tarbolton Path	6 B4		
Mossblown Street	6 B4	Tay Place	8 C7		
Mossgiel Lane (6)	8E6	Telford Avenue	8 E7		
Muir Street	6 C4	Thankerton Road	8 D6		
Muirshot Road	6 D3	Thistle Crescent	8 D5		
Myrtle Lane	8 D6	Tinto View Road	9 G7		
Nairn Street	6 B5	Tribboch Street	6 B4		
Ness Gardens	8 C7	Trinity Way (17)	8 E6		
Nethan Path	8 C7	Tweed Street	8 D6		
Netherburn Road	9 J7	Union Street	6 C4		
Nevison Street	8 D5	Victoria Court	6 C3		
Nikitas Avenue	8 D8	Victoria Street	6 C4		
North Street	6 C3	Wallace Drive	8 E5		
Nursery Drive	9 J7	Watson Street	6 B4		
Orchard Gate	8 C5	Waverley Street	8 C7		
Park View	8 D5	Wellbrae	8 C5		
Parker Place	6 D3	Wellgate Street	6 C3		
Parknook Way (6)	6 D3	West Clyde Street	8 D5		
Patchy Park	8 C7	West Fairholm Street	6 B2		
Pentland Crescent	6 B2	Westerton Avenue	8 D6		
Percy Street	6 C3	Whinknowe	9 H7		
Pitlochry Drive	8 E6	Whinnie Knowe	6 B6		
Portland Wynd (4)	6 D3	Wilkie Crescent	8 D5		
Powforth Close	6 A5	William Spiers Place	8 D6		
Primrose Avenue	8 C7	Willowbank	6 C2		
Prospect Drive	9 H7	Wilson Street	8 D6		

e Road 10 C1	Devon Gardens 10 C3	Kirkton Avenue 10 C3
Avenue 10 C2	Douglas Street 10 C3	Kirkton Court 10 C4
ew Place 10 C2	Dunard Court (1) 10 D2	Kirkton Street 10 D3
s Road 11 E4	East Avenue 10 B3	Laggan Road 10 D4
a Way 10 B3	Eastfield Road 11 E4	Lanark Road 10 D5
n Gardens 10 D4	Elderslea Road 11 E5	Langshaw Crescent 10 D3
n Place 10 D4	Elmbank Street 11 E5	Larksfield Drive 11 E5
Gardens 10 D5	Fleming Court 10 C4	Larkspur Way 10 D5
Avenue 10 C3	Forest Kirk 11 F5	Lavender Lane 10 C5
ore Avenue 11 E5	Forestlea Road 11 E5	Lawhill Place 10 A2
Lane 10 D2	Gair Crescent 11 E2	Leemuir View 11 F5
hfield Drive 11 E5	Gair Road 11 E1	Lochpark Avenue 10 D5
ane Gate 10 D2	Gasworks Road 10 A2	Lockhart Street 10 D3
ane Mews 11 E2	General Roy Way 11 G5	Luggie Road 10 B3
ane Park 10 D2	Gigha Gardens 11 E5	Malplaquet Court 11 F4
ane Road 10 D3	Gillbank Avenue 10 B3	Mandora Court 11 F4
y's Lane 10 D5	Glamis Avenue 10 D3	Marigold Way 10 D5
eld Loan 11 G4	Glenafeoch Road 10 E4	Market Place 10 D3
eld Place 11 G4	Glenburn Terrace 10 C5	Market Road 10 D3
Bull Close 10 D3	Glencoe Road 11 E4	Mauldslie Road 10 A3
heim Court 11 F4	Glendermott Court 10 D2	Mayfield Gardens 11 E6
bell Way 10 D5	Glenmavis Court 11 E4	Mayfield Place 11 E6
all Road 11 G6	Glenmavis Crescent 11 E4	Mayfield Toll 11 E5
well Road 10 C1	Goremire Road 10 E6	Meadow Court 11 G4
mar Crescent 11 E2	Goremire Road 10 G4	Melville Place 10 C3
end View 10 D4	Gowanside Place 10 B3	Middlehouse Court 10 B3
kbank Terrace 11 E4	Greenbank Terrace 10 D3	Mill Road 10 C4
rn Street 10 D2	Greenfield Road 10 D2	Miller Street 10 D3
anan Drive 11 G5	Hallcraig Place 10 B3	Milton Crescent 10 C4
Road 10 C2	Hamilton Street 10 D4	Milton Road 10 A5
bank Braes 10 D4	Hayward Court 11 G5	Milton Road 10 D5
on Lane 10 C3	Headsmuir Avenue 10 B3	Milton Street 10 C3
elhead Road 10 D6	Heather Row 10 C1	Moorside Street 10 E3
ban Court (2) 10 D2	Hemmingen Court 10 C2	Mossside Avenue 10 B3
eymount Road 10 D3	High Meadow 11 F5	Mount Stewart Street 10 C3
hill Court 11 E3	High Street 10 D3	Muirlee Road 11 F4
well Road 11 F5	Highmill Road 11 E3	Needle Green 10 D3
donia Gardens 10 C2	Hillfoot Terrace 11 E4	Neidpath Road 10 C2
eron Road 11 F5	Hillhead Avenue 11 E3	Newbarns Street 10 D2
eronian Drive 11 E4	Hillhouse Gate 11 G5	Newlands Terrace 10 D3
eluk Avenue 11 F5	Holm Street 10 C3	Nimmo Place 10 C2
n Lane 11 F4	Honeybank Crescent 10 E2	North Avenue 10 B3
wath Road 10 E4	Hope Street 11 E3	Northflat Place 11 G5
adale Gardens 11 E5	Howard Avenue 11 G5	Nursery Court 10 C2
anbuie Road 10 D2	Hozier Street 10 D3	Nursery Park 10 C3
ick Gardens 11 E5	Hyacinth Way 10D5	Old Bridgend 10 D4
land Avenue 10 D5	Islay Gardens 11 E5	Old Lanark Road 10 D4
sels Lane 10 D4	Ivanhoe Court 10 B4	Old Lanark Road 11 E6
sels Street 10 D3	Jackson Place 10 C2	Old Wishaw Road 10 C2
tlehill Road 10 C1	James Street 10 D4	Orchard Street 10 C4
tleknowe Gardens 10 C2	Jasmine Way 10 C5	Orion Way 10 B3
pel Street 10 D3	John Street 10 D4	Oudenarde Court 11 F4
rles Crescent 11 F4	Johnstone Lane 11 F4	Park Avenue 10 D2
stnut Grove 10 C4	Jonquil Way 10 D5	Park Circus 10 D2
rch Lane 10 D4	Jura Gardens 11 E5	Park Lane 10 C4
le Court 10 B3	Kelly's Lane 11 G4	Park Street 10 D4
le Street 10 B3	Kelso Drive 11 F4	Parkandarroch Crescent 11 E4
mbine Way 10 D5	Kenilworth Court 10 C4	Peacock Loan 10 D2
per Avenue 10 C2	Kenmore Way 10 D2	Pegasus Avenue 10 C3
runa Court 11 F4	Kilmartin Lane 10 D2	Primrose Way 10 C5
ignethan Road 10 C2	Kilmory Gardens 10 D2	Queen's Crescent 11 E3
thie Court 10 C2	Kilncadzow Road 11 G4	Ramage Road 11 F5
ssen Lane 11 F4	King's Crescent 11 E3	Ramillies Court 11 E4
ssmount Close 10 C3	Kintyre Wynd 10 D2	Rankin Gait 10 D3
nming Avenue 11 G5	Kirk Road 10 C3	Rankin Street 10 D3
idson Lane 11 F4	Kirk Street 10 C3	Redhouse Lane 10 D2
side Drive 11 E2	Kirkstyle Avenue 10 C4	St Lukes Avenue 10 C5

INDEX TO CARLUKE

Crescent	11 G5
Road	10 D3
Sanson Lane	11 G5
Sauchiesmoor Road (1)	11 E5
School Lane	10 C4
Shand Lane	10 D2
Shieldhill Road	10 C5
Skipness Avenue	11 E5
South Avenue	10 C3
Springfield Crescent	10 D5
Sraehouse Wynd	11 F4
Stanistone Road	11 E3
Station Road	10 C4
Stevenson Street	10 C3
Stewart Street	10 C2
Stirling Road	10 C1
Stonedyke Crescent	11 E2
Stonedyke Road	11 E2
Stonefield Gardens	10 D2
Strathlachlan Avenue	11 E4
Tantallon Court	10 C2
Tarbert Place	11 E4
Tayinloan Drive	11 F5
Thomson Street	10 D4
Thornlea Street	11 E5
Threave Court	10 C1
Union Street	10 D4
Unitas Crescent	10 C4
Victoria Avenue	10 C4
Violet Gardens	10 C5
Waterlands Gardens	11 E2
Weighhouse Road	10 C2
Weir's Lane	10 D3
West Avenue	10 B4
Westerhouse Court	10 B3
Whitehill Crescent	10 D2
Whiteshaw Avenue	10 B4
Whiteshaw Drive	10 B3
Wilton Road	11 E5
Windmill Gardens	10 D3
Windsor Court	10 D3
Windsor Quadrant	10 D3
Wisteria Lane	10 D5
Woodend Road	11 E3
Yieldshield Road	11 H4
Yvetot Court	10 C2